To Cha

MW01143838

hank you
Zachary's pen pal
and
pen pal
mom

AU-MAZING GIFT:

A Journey to Autism Acceptance

:')

Zachary

Dr. Alisha Griffith
Au.D CCC-SLP

Photography by Salih Abdur-Rahim,
Salih Hamilton Photography

Enjoy !!

Dr. Alisha Griffith

Table of Contents

DEDICATION

I dedicate this book to my mini heartbeat, Zachary. You are an Au-mazing Gift, that touches the world with your smile, kind heart and captivating personality. You make the world a better place. You make ME a better person. Thank you for teaching me the art of patience, listening and most importantly how to love, beyond limits.

To my mom or wind beneath my wings, I appreciate all of your support, help with raising Zachary and endless love. I appreciate your spiritual guidance and continuous encouragement. I love you both, to the moon and back.

INTRODUCTION

I'm sure that as you picked up this book you're searching for answers. I applaud you for your courage to step outside of the confusion, the pain, and the overwhelming feeling you had upon learning that your child has been diagnosed with autism. The word "autism" is usually like an overwhelming flood. I know that right now it may feel like a wave that's going to drown you, that you can't come out from. More than anything, I want you to know that you are not alone. This is not a curse. Your child is different, but I promise you this wonderful, precious gift that you brought into the world is still the gift that you've been given.

I want to talk to you about how to truly embrace this unique gift. I know what it's like. My son has been diagnosed as being on the autism spectrum, and he is 10 years old now. Even though as an Audiologist and Speech Language Pathologist working with children who are on the Autism Spectrum daily, discovering that my child was "autistic" caused a crushing weight. I wasn't sure I could have handled this hitting so close to home. I soon began to learn that, this "autism" is a gift that I was given. I want to help you really embrace your child as a precious, wonderfully unique person.

CHANGE OF HEART

My hard working parents are from Guyana, South America. They came to the United States of America on a scholarship to pursue their graduate studies at Oklahoma State University. Apparently I was part of their studies, because I was born in Stillwater, Oklahoma while they were there. We then moved back to Guyana when I was 3 years old. Shortly after they divorced and I lived there until I was eight. My mother, older brother and I later returned to the United States and lived in Brooklyn, New York.

I attended the State University of New York at Stony Brook, where I received my undergraduate education. Originally, I entered college with a desire

12

for sciences and to become a pediatrician, until I encountered the dreaded "Organic Chemistry." I received my first and only "D" with this class. At that time, I realized that my wanting to become a medical doctor was really not my primary interest. It was that of my father, who no longer lived with us. I remember as a little girl hearing him say, "I want my children to become doctors". Facing this feeling of being a "failure" in my father's eyes, I began to take a wide array of classes towards my undergraduate degree in Social Sciences Interdisciplinary, with a minor in Child and Family Studies. This began my personal search to figure out what did "I" really want to be when I grow up. My early thoughts of becoming a teacher was no longer my focus. I accidentally stumbled into a class called "The Special Child." At first, I thought it was going to be just another introductory level class. I didn't expect that this experience would help in shaping my life to where I am today. As I sat in this class, listening and absorbing what it is to be a special child, I became so intrigued. It was amazing to me to learn about the concept of people who were "dis" abled, who were not fully functioning and yet they were still able.

I remember how much of an impact it made on me. I went home and told my mom, "I want to work with these people. They're amazing. They're people, just like us. They're just not able to do as much as some of us can, but something about when you see them smile and how they can light up an entire room." I had a change of heart.

I began my career working in the field for children with special needs, initially as a direct care worker. Then as a recreation therapist, case manager and later as a special education teacher in the classroom. I reflect on my role as a direct care worker, I was first assigned to Heidi, a sweet young woman with multiple disabilities. Heidi was non-verbal, non-ambulatory and needed help in meeting her daily needs. The first time that I assisted her with her bath was filled of challenges. She was not able to verbally communicate with me and I had limited skills on how to interact with her. I continued to work with her over time and we developed a close bond. My time away from her was filled with searching for ways to better meet her needs to enhance her daily functioning. I also learned about the value of having patience, when working with her. She became a major influence for my graduate studies in Communication. I continued my education in Speech Language Pathology and eventually earned my doctorate in Audiology. My father did eventually get his wish fulfilled by me, since he didn't specify what kind of "doctor"☺. This all became an integral part of my life's journey, filled with experiences that have been enlightening.

Then my son was born. He was a bundle of joy that we took pleasure in welcoming into the family. He was also the first grandchild. At first, he was on target with his developmental milestones, walking, running and jumping around the house. By the age of 2, we prepared him for out of home care to pre-school. He received more immunization shots for schooling and was given a few at each visit, at that time. Soon after, things began to change. I saw the signs, but was in strong denial at first. I thought to myself. "Not my child". Autism was not something that I wanted for my child. I didn't want him to have the challenges that I saw daily at work. I began my quest for information on a personal level. It was a long journey from denial to acceptance. I learned and now believe in my heart that our Au-mazing children are God's angels sent for us and others, here in the world.

CONNECT WITH YOUR CHILD

I encourage you to connect with your au-mazing child. I know from experience that connection does not rely entirely on how much training you have, and how much knowledge you possess on the subject. It is important that you establish a deep and meaningful connection with your child. I want to help you to understand that there is no shame in the au-some gift that your child is. They are uniquely special just as they are. They may have challenges that you didn't consider nor predict that they would have while growing up, but that doesn't make them less than, it just makes them who they are. Your child may appear isolated from others, but I guarantee you that they are still connected to you and to their external world. Every au-mazing child, in their own unique and special way, wants to be connected to their mothers.

Zachary has a deep fascination with Thomas the Tank Engine and friends. He knows each one by their name and unique features. He would become frustrated when he couldn't find one or if he could not bring them with him. A way of me establishing our connection was to sit, play and engage in conversations about the trains with him. He would communicate more when it was of his interest and we would connect in this way. Sometimes, I would link things that happened to Thomas to what is happening around Zachary and this would help him to connect more with real life situations.

This can be the hardest part for us, as moms. We want them to connect with us in "our" way and focus on our topics in which they may share no interest. There are days when we want so badly to give our children a hug and want them to hug us back. Sometimes, we just want to sit and have a conversation with them, but our children may not want to, and in some cases this may not be a choice for them. What I know for sure, is that this doesn't make them un-able. We will experience them being "differently able". In other words, they will love, communicate and interact differently. We have to discover how to get into our children's worlds and connect with them to know who they truly are. It's important to not impose your own world view onto your children. Be open and receptive to listening, learning, accept and understand their views. It's hard for us because we try to push our children to be "normal." You look at them, and everything in your heart wants your child to be just like the other kids at the playground.

I know there are times when my son goes to the playground and wants to run with lightning speed, spin around in circles, or get on the swing and swing back and forth, repeatedly. I had to learn that his definition of fun may not be the "same" as the other children there. He may not be interested in the group or organized play that the "other" children are doing. I had to learn to accept that, he's going to be himself, and play the way he wants to play, and even though it may look different from the outside view, he is having fun playing and that's priceless. That was my "AHA" moment.

When I started to accept his au-mazing gift of accepting and allowing him to be himself and stopped wanting him to be anyone else.

As we start to accept our children and we stop the comparisons, we can find freedom, and joy, as we learn to love them for them. Maybe sometimes, they don't want to play with the other kids. That's okay. If you release that need to compare, you can find and will see that joy in their eyes as they are allowed to completely be themselves. You will see the smile on their faces and the light in their eyes, as they feel accepted being allowed to be themselves, and do whatever it is that brings them joy. You will also see their gift of connection and how their joy transfers to others around them.

If you have other children, and only one child is on the Autism spectrum, it's easy to want to compare, as the sibling grows and advances more rapidly. We have to accept who they are and stop trying to make them who we think they should be. As you release the toxic negativity for desiring "normal" from your au-mazing child, you will change your mindset into positive energy and that's when true freedom will occur. When we learn to change our mindset to accept, connect and engage in their worlds, it becomes refreshing and feels like a breath of fresh air.

FACING CHALLENGES

There are challenges that we will have to face that other parents don't have. For example, going to a birthday party can be hard for our au-mazing children. Zachary gets so excited with the idea of going to birthday parties, but all of these people in one place can be overstimulating and that can be a very difficult situation for him, and myself at times. There are ways to still have this experience be enjoyable for our kids. Consider going a little bit earlier or ask the mom of the birthday child if there can be a designate area at the party with less kids and lower stimulation. Therefore, they can be there with the other kids, but perhaps off to the side. That way they can still be in that cool party area but not have to be in the middle of it. Then maybe other kids can come over and play with them, as we have experienced. Give them the opportunity to be able to experience that party, but still be okay with their individual needs. Let them use that little bit of separation that they need. There's nothing wrong with that.

Your child is going to experience the party differently. You may need to go early and you may even need to leave earlier. Observe your child for signs of fatigue, or when they are simply changing gears and showing signs that it's time to move on. That's just simply what your unique child needs. I'll tell you a secret: when you start looking at children who are living with autism without judgment, without preconceived notions, and instead just allow them to be themselves, you'll see a level of happiness in your child that often does not exist in normal kids. When we stop comparing them to others, we can find that there is this special kind of joy that these precious angels have.

As a mom of an au-mazing child, there are practical things that you need to do. You need to find ways to allow them to have this joy; it may be something as simple as flipping a piece of paper that makes them so happy. There are also times when they want to go outside to play but we don't allow them to do so because we want to protect them from the stares of others or their comments. It's okay if your parenting looks different. You have to do what is best for you and your child.

I now know my son is my angel. Yes, he lives with autism, but he is perfect to me. It's hard for us as humans because we were raised from a very young age to judge what is supposed to be normal because we just see things based on what our eyes can see. I encourage you to let go of the challenges of what you see and embrace what you feel. Does it feel normal? Does your child experience joy in their way? When you stop and you open your eyes, ears and hearts to their joy, you will accept your child without limits. No one wants their child to be different. Let's work on shifting our mindsets and learning to embrace their differences.

DENIAL TO ACCEPTANCE

I remember the lowest point in my life. It was that day that I got the diagnosis. I saw the signs in him and, as a professional in the field, I knew clearly what those signs were. I didn't want it to be true. I wasn't going to say it out loud. As Zachary got ready to go to his next level of preschool, I knew that I needed to get him tested so he could get the services that he needed. As he was being evaluated, I observed his challenges in staying focused and seated. I also remember watching the test administrator's responses to the answers he was giving. I was familiar with these responses because I had given similar tests countless times to other children, but I still had a hard time accepting it with "my' child. My waiting period for the results of the test over the weeks was filled with anxiety. I was a nervous wreck, even though many did not know what I was going through. I walked around with a smile on the outside but felt like my inside world was crumbling apart. I received the envelope with the test results and the paper inside with the letters boldly written, PDD-NOS (Pervasive Developmental Disorder- Not Otherwise Specified, which is a diagnosis used for children with milder symptoms on the Autism Spectrum). I felt everything around me stopped; seeing it in print made it so real.

I remember sitting there crying while holding the paper in my hands. In a flash, I saw what our whole life was going to be like. Right in that instant, I gave up on how I thought his life would look, or at least that's how it felt. All of my dreams when I was pregnant and all of my preconceived notions of him being a doctor disappeared. I desperately needed a mindset shift because I was at an all-time low. After surrounding myself with personal transformation and development classes, books and strong, unique influencers, I began to shift my perspective to positivity in my life throughout. I began my transition from denial to acceptance of his unlimited possibilities and options in his future.

I took comfort and received that my son is on the curve of the Autism Spectrum. He is abled "differently" to accomplish many things. He is in a class with a smaller amount of children in a regular public school and benefits from a team of skilled and caring professionals. He's now about a grade or two behind the other kids in learning. He deals with some cognitive learning issues and works at a slower pace with the help of a para-professional in class to help him with his focus. I may have had to let go of my dreams for his future, but it didn't mean he wouldn't live a joyful, healthy life and be allowed to go after "his" dream of what he wants to be. His dream includes him "seeing the world."

SEEKING HELP

The process of developing a strong co-parent and support network has been a critical aspect of this Au-mazing journey. When he was three months old, his father and I separated and later divorced. We proceeded to co-parent and had some issues around accepting the diagnosis and label of "Autism" as well as the huge financial responsibilities involved with caring for a child on the spectrum. Although Zachary and I were grateful for the physical help he provided on an on-going basis, more financial help was needed. Zachary's financial needs began to increase as he got older.

At that time, I was looking for help in all forms, by trying proposed treatments and remedies that were recommended. Some of the options I tried, using natural and organic fruits and foods, chiropractic treatments, homeopathic remedies, and so much more that I researched that I thought would make my child feel "better" and help him live the best life possible. This was costly and it became harder to do it with limited financial support.

My lowest point occurred when I walked into the city's Child Support Office and began the process to get on-going child support for Zachary, since this was not part of the divorce settlement. My heart felt so heavy but my mind knew that Zachary's needs were becoming greater and continuous financial support from his dad was now more necessary. I remember sitting there in the court and saying to myself, "I can't believe I'm here! But my son requires so much." I said out loud to the judge, "My son has special needs!" That was the first time I ever said that out loud in public. I had to show the judge the bills and receipts for treatments and lifestyle changes that he was currently receiving.

The judge said, "Can you guys work this out? There is no way that a mom can do this alone. Your child has special needs. Can you work it out?"

This was one of the most difficult situations I had to go through. So I know how difficult your low moments can be, but I promise you that there is light on the other side.

We were able to meet outside of the court amicably and child support was fairly decided on with the help of his lawyer, helping our process.

Establishing my extensive support network, which includes his dad, my mom and step dad (that are always there to lend support) and help with the relief of when a mommy break is needed. My brother, sisters and cousins continue to help with acceptance and being patient when spending time with Zachary. My friends and family members continue to embrace and connect with Zachary through our shared events, travel and occasions. They have helped me in this process of using and maximizing our village to help the world of "Autism" not feel so isolated.

Today we are incredibly blessed to be able to provide Zachary with therapies (such as Speech and Occupational), socialization martial arts therapy for kids on the spectrum (called So SMART Kids, which is a program that my partner Shihan Phil and I created to meet the needs of more Au-mazing children), specialized tutoring and afterschool activities and so much more to help Zachary learn be the most productive member of society that he can be. I am thankful to have a supportive network and team that helps with this Au-mazing journey.

I wanted you to understand that your "au-mazing" gift, was hand selected and given to you, purposefully. You have what it takes within you to connect and created a meaningful relationship with this child. And even when times are hard and you feel clueless or even failing as a parent, you are not alone on this Au-mazing journey. Look at your gift, be grateful and SMILE.

TEN

A.U.M.A.Z.I.N.G.L.Y

SUCCESSFUL TOOLS FOR

YOUR JOURNEY TO

AUTISM ACCEPTANCE

1. ACCEPT DIFFERENCES

Accept the difference in you and you will embrace the difference in the world

I always knew I was different. I purposely chose to do things differently.

While everyone cheered for the popular, the less popular was more interesting to me. As my friends around me chose to study and become medical doctors and lawyers, I chose a field like Audiology (balance and hearing loss), for my doctoral studies. Audiology is a different and less favored field of study. So when graced with Zachary, learning to embrace his quirkiness and loving on his individuality of what made him "different", began my acceptance process. We can get caught up with the way society have placed a negative view on "being different." If we really think about it, we "all" are different. So who or what determines the level of acceptance in regards to the spectrum of difference in society? How about we start to accept the differences in the world, specifically the differences within the spectrum of autism, and present to the world that "differences" is absolutely Au-mazing?

A. Differently-abled.

Differently- able emphasizes that there are abilities that exists and should be nurtured. Identify what are your child's "different" skills. As we stop comparing our "unique child" to other children and start highlighting their individual actions and progress, we begin to appreciate their different abilities. Each child develops and can make their individual progress over time, once actions, effort and practice is put into place.

B. Its different outside the box.

While I was pregnant, I had a dream and vision for Zachary. I had expectations of what he would do, see and become. When we place expectations on our children's lives, we sometimes place them in a box (an imaginary place with 4 imaginary walls). When their actions are "different" from our expectations, we tend to become disappointed. As you learn to think and live outside of the box, and support them as they step out of the box, you begin to feel less constricted, less disappointed and more excited for their possibilities.

C. Think different, do different, be different.

It's okay to think differently than anyone else. Children on the spectrum, have unique perspectives and that's refreshing from the norm. Do different, because the same is expected and in my opinion, boring and predictable. Imagine if we all had to eat the same foods, without different flavors or spices, every day? Being different is what the world is made up of, variety in individuals is beautiful. Are you ready to declare to the world? "The beauty of my child is how he/she thinks differently, do differently and IS different!"

2. UNIQUE STRENGTHS

Focus more on the individual strengths than weaknesses

You have strengths and qualities within you that separates you from everyone else. Identifying your strengths as a parent helps with coping and acceptance. Use your strengths to help your child and also to help others. As we help others more, we begin to truly identify our role in this journey of being the parent to your child. Identify your child's strengths also. Identify what they enjoy doing that makes them absolutely au-mazing. Recognize that we each have our individual unique blueprint.

I have worked with Au-mazing children that have demonstrated strengths that would have been missed if I chose to only focus on limitations. Some of the strengths I have noticed over my time includes, observing incredible details, sharp memory, ability to make others around them smile or laugh, creativity with their hands, putting together objects starting from scratch, and so much more.

Here are some factors that may help you to identify strengths

A. What does he or she like to do?
B. What are the things that your child can do amazingly well?
C. Encourage them to show or tell you and others what they can do.
D. Pay attention to the compliments people say about your child.

E. Who are their favorite people and where are their favorite places to go?

As we start to identify our strengths and our child's strengths, we can learn to create a bridge to connect them. For example, my strengths include connecting and communicating with others. Zachary's strengths include making others around him smile and laugh. Together we sit down and connect by telling each other jokes. This is just one example of how focusing on strengths can "strengthen" your bond with your children. What are some cool things that you do as a family that fosters and supports your child's strengths?

3. MINDSET SHIFT

Shift from negative thinking to Positive Energy Power

Mindset shifting has been one of the most impactful methods that have helped with my acceptance of Zachary being my Au-mazing gift. Shifting your mindset can be used in all aspects of your life, especially when it involves how we interact with others, including our children. This is an effective method of parenting that can be introduced in all households.

I have spent time in all of Kubler-Ross, Elizabeth (1969). 5 stages of grief, which includes denial, anger, bargaining, depression and acceptance. As I began to become more in tune with myself to become more aware that we go through these stages when dealing with major situations in our lives any time. We must give ourselves permission to recognize and work through the process of each stage as we visit and sometimes "revisit" the previous stages. The concept of going from toxic negativity to positive energy power, described in detail by one of my mentors Edith Namm, founder of Share-a-Smile Ambassadors, books called *Change to a Positive Mindset and extend your Lifeline: A Journey to Miles of Smiles, Positive Energy Power, Hope Health and Happiness*

I have spoken to parents about their experiences with the stages of grief over time. Denial and anger seems to occur the longest and most frequently in families with children living with Autism.

I have heard responses that ranges from "why me", "why would God do this to me" or "what did I do to deserve this"?

In fact, one of the main reasons I wrote this book is because of how often I have heard these questions. If we continue to stay in the, "woe is me" and the "why me" state, then we will remain stuck in the negative zone. As you start shifting your thoughts to more of love, gratuity, compassion, creating a peaceful environment, and good self-images for yourself and your child, it will increase the positive input in your life. You will start to develop answers to your why me. You will become more aware that you were given a gift, who is your child. You will also learn to teach and model to your child to have a more positive mindset.

A. *Denial to Acceptance.*

We all have experienced going through the 5 stages of Grief, with different circumstances, including that of being an Au-mazing parent. Denial, Anger, Bargaining, Depression and Acceptance, can occur within any unforeseen time throughout our journey and that's okay. It's okay to experience feeling angry, frustrated and disappointment, shucks I know I have revisited them a few times, even within a 24-hour period. However, it is important that we don't remain in the first 4 stages for an extended time. Through positive lifestyle practices, we can learn to create opportunities around us that will allow you to smile more and be more appreciative. If you recognize that you are challenged with making your shift to positive, consult your support team or get professional help as soon as possible.

B. Light in your life.

AUTISM is not YOUR fault, or anyone else's. Understand every child will have their have their own unique situations to endure and to overcome. It's important for us to identify the blessings and lessons. There is a light that illuminates from their eyes and souls. Find the joy in their lightness. Observe how your child brings light to those around them and try to do the same. I have seen Zachary enter a room and shifted the energy with his light, his pure self and being.

C. Shift from mindless to mindful.

Far too often we get caught up in the immediate, or start to get over concerned with the future. Remember to be mindful to take one day at a time. Be patient, to trust and believe that all will be well. I completely understand that sometimes it doesn't feel that way, but when we start trusting and place our faith in a higher being that is bigger than us, I call him GOD, ALL of the responsibility for knowing all of the unknown answers fall off our shoulders.

I believe when we trust, believe, have faith in GOD (or whomever you may call your Creator) and remain in positive energy action, our children's futures will be ignited. Take a deep breath and release the worry, they will be okay. Start practicing mindset shift exercises, using positive thoughts, words and actions in your daily lives. Use positive affirmations with your child daily.

One positive daily shifting routine we do in our home as we brush our teeth in the mornings, we both look in the mirror and say out loud "I AM A WINNER" then smile ☺. This begins our joint mindset shift for the rest of the day. What are some positive daily shifting activities can you include in your routines?

4. ATTACH AND CONNECT

Give your children the attention they need.

You, as the parent, model how to engage with others through demonstration and by putting into practice. Even though "au" in Autism indicates the solo nature of the child. It doesn't start and end there. By modeling and actively engaging with your child daily, it allows them to "see" and later "do" joint activities with you and others. Children do as they see and hear.

A. Be present in this moment.

Spend time with your child (create a visual reminder if you need). Remove distractions, like televisions and phones. Try to maintain a daily routine where you get to connect and engage doing something that you both love to do. For example, have a weekly date night/morning. Choose places they like. Try to include a place you like every once in a while.

B. Bridge the gap.

Slowly introduce and include something you like so that it will feel authentic. We can connect with our feelings. Enter their world. If they sing and play with specific toys, then get on their level and play with the same objects.

C. Smile, laugh and be silly together

(communicate and connect). Too often we forget that being silly together is another manner of engaging. Embrace the child in you and have your inner child bond with your child. The power of a smile goes very far. Have fun together, it's one of the strongest "glue".

5. ZESTFUL LIVING

Find ways to help to reduce your stress levels daily

.

So often we forget the importance of self- care, self-love and self- preservation. What actions are we doing to preserve our minds, bodies and inner-souls? We spend the majority of the day taking care and advocating for others, scheduling appointments with doctors and therapists, we forget to put on our oxygen mask first. Breathe. Being a parent to an au-mazing child, can require a lot of our time and energy. We must remember to set aside time for ourselves daily, weekly, monthly and yearly, even if you have to place it on your schedule to make it happen, do it. Release the countless excuses of why you cannot do it, like money, time, energy and more excuses that come so easily. How can you create and practice the art of stress release?

A. Set aside a few minutes daily to reset.

Try actions like prayer, meditation, reflections, reading a book and/or writing. Practice writing or speaking out loud examples of what you are grateful for help yourself by scheduling private time alone and with friends.

B. Take care of your body and it will take care of you.

Take walks or go to the gym consistently. Take classes such as cardio-kickboxing, martial arts (one of my personal favorites), yoga, body conditioning, even fun classes like Zumba and belly dancing. One of my clients raves about the way she feels after a belly dancing or African dance class. Doing it alone is great, or you may prefer to have a work out buddy for motivation and support. Either way get to moving, it's great for the body, taking care of your health and your soul, just having those minutes where the focus is primarily, YOU.

C. Continue to do the things you enjoy.

Remember to still honor and treat yourself with time off (vacation or a night away without the kids). Part of what keeps me sane are my traveling adventures with my girlfriends to international countries. The time that I set aside are so precious that I appreciate that time and always look forward to stepping back into my Au-mazing mom role. It is important to be in gratitude, move your body and do something enjoyable each day.

6. I MATTER

It is your responsibility to spread awareness and acceptance.

Sometimes I feel like I live in a microscope and others are watching, judging and at times criticizing what we do. One mom, in my Facebook support group, called "Moms connect with their Au-mazing child", said her son has moments when it becomes difficult for her to manage his behavior like hitting, biting or refusal to go places during transit. The stares and the comments she gets from others around her when this occurs, she said "is so disheartening and makes her angry". She feels that they are judging her to be a "bad mother" because of what they see. "Instead of asking if they can help in any way, they stare and make negative comments."

Autism Awareness Month is in April and because of major organizations and more public information, people are becoming more aware that Autism exists now. Our reality is that awareness is not the same as understanding and acceptance and many still lack the knowledge and understanding of what it looks like during everyday life functions. I believe that as Au-mazing parents, we can help to spread the concepts of Autism acceptance and understanding. We can show the world that our children are "differently abled" and should be included and accepted. How will you help to increase the sensitivity and the compassion to the world of Autism? How can you show that "I" matter in your community?

A. Educate others and shine a light on what our lives truly look like.

Show how our daily lives and situations differ because of having children with "Autism". Inform others that it is a wide spectrum and that no two children on the Autism Spectrum are the same, even though they have similar characteristics. Show them how they can include an Au-mazing family into "their" world. Education can be done through talking, writing, postings on social media, and increased attention in media by having shows /programs that highlights more about our lives. The mini-series on the Oxygen TV Network, "For Peete's Sake" was one of the most recent examples of this where the audience learned more about Autism in their households. Imagine if we had more shows like that, especially with everyday families like you and I? The world would be more connected and compassionate on the reality of living with Autism.

B. Let others know how we feel.

Explain to them things to say and do with us and things "not to say" and do with us. Instead of speaking during anger and frustration as a response, speak up and inform BEFORE. As you begin to feel more comfortably speaking about yourself and your journey, they will begin to have more compassion and increase what they know. We are the authors of our story. Our stories will then impact how they react. I feel like it is up to us to help them to understand so that they can start teaching "their children" from childhood, the importance of including Au-mazing children at school, on the playground in their lives.

C. **Shifting from guilt to acceptance**.

It really starts with ourselves and how we perceive the situation that we are in. How do we look at our Au-mazing children? Do we see them as what they truly are, which are specially wrapped unique gifts ☺? Can we see and feel the Au- mazing and Au- some ness in Autism? Now, can we introduce this perception to others, so they can also share the beauty within it. Instead of having difficulty bringing your child places because you are afraid of judgments or comments by others, start small, and with areas that your child will be more comfortable, that have less crowds and less noise. Be able to tell others that your child is on the autism spectrum. Be more vocal about it and open to sharing more about the journey. Take back your power and your voice, because the world truly needs it. It wasn't until I started letting more people know about my Zachary, that random people, completely unexpected would speak to me privately about their experiences with Autism (some were parents, family members and others who knew other families). It began to become easier for them talk about it, which increases understanding and compassion. The key to the transformation of others is when your story has a positive life supporting theme, because you matter.

7. NOISE MAKERS

Let the world know that we are here.

This whole process can be scary, from pre-diagnosis, to formal diagnosis to the, present and what now moments to the planning of the future. There is the noise of the outside world, with comments, sometimes negative, about Autism. We also have our internal chatter, the noise of our own self-doubt, fear, anger and joy. When I released the need to be the "perfect mom" and started to believe that I was doing the best that I can do, was the moment I began to feel less pressure from the outside world. I began to place less demands on myself and Zachary.

Learn as much as you can about the Autism Spectrum using all your resources, including written information, organizations, professionals and parents that have gone through what you are currently experiences. The more informed you are, the greater noise you can make.

A. You are your child's loudest bullhorn.

Step out from fear and grow in courage through informing yourself and then informing others. Also, learn to trust your intuition. I have tried my best to make clear and informed decisions and sometimes I have learned to rely on my gut or plain intuition, as a mother. Make noise when it matters, in fact make noise whenever you can, especially as it comes to being your child's advocates at home, school or in the environment. Continue to build your confidence as a strong advocate for your child and others on the Autism spectrum.

B. The world may have many negative things to say and will judge.

Meet their negativity with positivity. They are individuals out there that are ignorant and lack the desire to learn more about Autism. If you are surrounded by that energy and "meanness", first try to educate them with facts and positive aspects. If they are still negative, it may be time to remove yourself, and definitely your child, from their toxicity. They are simply not worth it.

C. **Clarify the myths**.

They say your child is Autism? My child is NOT Autism. He shows characteristics that are on the Autism Spectrum. Our children are more than the diagnosis. The diagnosis helps to understand their behavior and actions, but it doesn't determine who they are as an individual. They are so many more dynamic characteristics that exists, let's identify and embrace them also. First love them for who they are. I tell everyone, Zachary is very energetic, has the biggest heart and shows so much care for others around him. He loves to swim, travel and play with his trains. He is also on the Autism Spectrum, where sometimes he prefers to have less interaction with others and is "working on" being more sociable. Therefore, I emphasize his strengths and passion first, then give additional information to help others to understand him more that may relate to him being on the spectrum, like he hums and whirls his arms like a helicopter when he's excited, has a deep fascination with Thomas the Tank Engine and friends and may have a short attention span when speaking to him. I may share this so that others understand him more, can connect with him, and not fee offended if he chooses not to connect with you, and to avoid judgements.

8. GO BIG

Have goals and go after them

My mother has always instilled in me that the sky is my limit, to go after whatever I want with pride and momentum. I attribute a lot of who I am today based on the strong support and encouragement that I receive from her. It was not always easy, as she raised me mostly as a single parent, mostly working two jobs to make sure my brother and I got what we wanted. Today she remains steadfast in supporting us to go after our biggest dreams and goals. As we set our goals and chase after them, it is our duty to provide our children with the support that they need to be the most productive and their best self that they can be. Are you allowing your child to dream big and supporting them to go after it?

A. Find out their dreams, goals and passions.

Look at their strengths and the things that they enjoy doing consistently over time. Blend with what we see that make them smile on the inside. Listen to what they say they say that they would like to do. Even if it sounds unrealistic and impossible, encourage them to start making the necessary steps that they are capable of doing. Help them to plan and most importantly foster their belief in themselves.

B. Help create a vision board for you and for your child.

This is a fun activity to do with your child. It allows you into their world. It helps to set visual, and possibly verbal, intentions. It's a bonding exercise also.

C. All children have dreams.

It doesn't matter what end of the spectrum; our children may function within. We can instill important values like self-belief, self-worth and trying your best. Support your child's dreams, even as zany as some may sound.

9. LEARN TO LISTEN

Listen with our ears, eyes and heart.

As an Audiologist, I have always been fascinated with the science of hearing and the art of listening. There is a distinct difference between hearing and listening. Most of us spend the majority of time hearing. Start practicing the art of listening by adding understanding and meaning to what is being said.

Zachary tells others clearly that his name is Z-A-C-H-A-R-Y, Zachary, not Zach, Zee, Zachy (or any other endearing shortenings). He doesn't like to be called any shortened versions, or nicknames, because he said that's not his name. He wants to be heard and listened to. What is your child really telling you through their words or actions that you may have missed before? What are some ways that you can improve your listening?

A. Listen with our ears

Practice patience and really listen to what your child is saying. Ignore what others or society's expectations about your child. Listen to what your child wants and needs. Listen as they express their ideas and dreams. They will clearly tell you what they like and don't like. Sometimes it may not come out sounding soft and smooth and maybe perceived harsh, or honest yet blunt. It is important for us to remove limitations placed on them by society's expectations and support.

B. Listen with our eyes.

Be aware of what you see. Especially in the silence. Observe facial expressions, body language and tune into non-verbal clues, as well as yours. Look your child in the eyes when speaking. Even though they may look away and avoid prolonged eye contact. Most of the time they need to know that you are present and visibly there. As a working mom, I have struggled with not being always there for everything with Zachary. I have released the guilt and pressure by treasuring the extra moments when we are together to bond through strengthening our listening to each other.

C. Listen with an open heart and an open mind.

Know what makes them smile and happy by paying attention. Allow the possibilities for the range of emotions that will be displayed. Try to put yourself in their shoes by looking at each situation through their perspectives. Be alert and aware of what upsets and angers them so we can predict possible incidences or occurrences. Listening with an open mind, by being a few steps ahead of your child will help to avoid major meltdowns.

10. YOU ARE NOT ALONE

There IS SUPPORT for you along this journey

It took me almost 8 years to be comfortable to say that my son was on the Autism Spectrum, out loud. A few of my closest family members and friends knew but the majority didn't. As he grew older, I got bolder. I had to learn to say it out loud, to myself and to others. Accepting that the support that was given around me, such as family, friends and so many extensions, was a blessing and much needed help. I had to get out of my own way of thinking I had to handle it all alone and the mis-conception "no-one else can take care of my child." Learned to say "yes, I need your help" and "yes, I need a shoulder to cry on right now."

I am grateful to speak and work with countless families and I am realizing that they are many mothers out there that are just like me. They have kept that information to themselves and didn't speak to others about how Autism impacted them personally. We have a tendency to hold things in and think that no one else understands. If we start to understand that we don't have to face this alone then we can start to help other families impacted by Autism. I also began to really receive the message and trust that our Creator sends other "helpers" to help us take care of his special "angels".

A. Parents need support after their child is first diagnosed.

This is one of the most critical periods and time, the immediate time after receiving the diagnosis. This immediate post-diagnosis period has been described to me, by another mother as feeling like a pin being stuck into your balloon, deflated. This type of support can be access to professionals (like social workers, doctors, therapists, etc.). These individuals can provide the informational support.

B. Select another parent that has walked a similar path.

There are tough days when our children may have melt downs, shut downs or even unexplainable behavior that we simply don't understand. There also will be exciting days when you want to share successes, wins and achievements that you will want to share with someone who really understands. Having role models or parents that have been there before helps because they can relate through their similar personal experiences. It's very important to have this support available to us. Other mothers that have walked this path have helped me by providing information on programs, services, **and provided extra strength and emotional support in times of need**. Some of these role models can be found in physical support groups (like how I connected with Michelle), schools' parents groups, social media group forums. I created a Facebook group called "Moms connect with Au-mazing children" as a place where we can share our stories. I have seen and have received so much information from my So SMarT Kids, moms. During and after classes, I would see them chatting and laughing as they share information and stories.

C. *Build your "support team."*

This team may include family members, friends, professionals, therapists and coaches that can provide assistance to the improvement on your overall lives. Surround yourself with other positive energies. My support team consists of my mom, stepdad, sisters, brother, cousins, close friends, teachers and therapists, and a few other Au-mazing mothers that I have met along the path. I am truly grateful to have them for all for their continued advice, help and genuine love.

Accepting my GIFT

My mentors, Edith Namm, Susie Carder and my mom, helped me to understand that my life was designed and created in purpose. It was time for me to accept and share my gifts, with the path that was given to me. Starting earlier, with my deep interest to work with children with "exceptional" needs and on the spectrum, then expanding to children *and* families with communication needs and finally gifted with my very own au-mazing son. My vision is to share and help other Au-mazing moms, like me, shift their mindsets to positive parenting and to create deeper connections with their children. Helping them to go from disconnected and lonely, to experiencing increased communication and deeper engagements with their precious gifts.

Once we incorporate these 10 A. U. M. A. Z. I. N. G. L. Y useful tools into our daily lives, we can spread acceptance and inclusion of Autism, globally. Practice of these tools helps us to learn to *accept our "differences"* and recognize our *unique strengths. Shift our mindsets* to positive thinking and start *making noise* about the Spectrum, everywhere and in every type of platform possible. I truly believe that *we matter* as parents, and our children matter, as we *attach and connect* and live our life with *zest*, we can make a major impact on the world's perception. You can do this through encouraging each other to *go after big dreams* and by *listening* to what others around you are thinking, saying and doing. This will help you to really appreciate your Au-mazing gifts. Remember, *you are not alone* in this journey. There is support around you.

Are you ready to open your arms, minds and hearts, to receiving it?

Alisha Griffith (July 29, 2016).pdf

Open

Extract

Open with

Details

Comments

4 of 8

Book Alisha Griffith (July 29, 2016).pdf

Book_

References

1. Kulber-Ross, Elisabeth (1969). On Death on Death and Dying

Namm, E. & Kaufman R. (2011). *Change to a Positive Mindset and Extend your Lifeline: A Journey to Miles of Smiles, Positive Energy Power, Hope, Health and Happiness*

Made in the USA
Middletown, DE
28 September 2016